A STEP-BY-STEP
TRAINING
COCKATIELS

ELAINE RADFORD

Photographers: Rebecca Brega, Isabelle Francais, Michael Gilroy, E. Gold-finger, Bruce D. Lavoy, Ron and Val Moat, Horst Mueller, N. Richmond, Vince Serbin, T. Tilford, Dr. M.M. Vriends, Wayne Wallace, R. Williams.

Title page: Headstudy of a lutino Cockatiel. The delightful personality and charming appearance of the Cockatiel has made this little parrot one of the most popular cage birds in the world.

Humorous drawings by Andrew Prendimano.

Distributed in the UNITED STATES by T.F.H. Publications, Inc., One T.F.H. Plaza, Neptune City, NJ 07753; in CANADA to the Pet Trade by H & L Pet Supplies Inc., 27 Kingston Crescent, Kitchener, Ontario N2B 2T6; Rolf C. Hagen Ltd., 3225 Sartelon Street, Montreal 382 Quebec; in CANADA to the Book Trade by Macmillan of Canada (A Division of Canada Publishing Corporation), 164 Commander Boulevard, Agincourt, Ontario M1S 3C7; in ENGLAND by T.F.H. Publications Limited, Cliveden House/Priors Way/Bray, Maidenhead, Berkshire SL6 2HP, England; in AUSTRALIA AND THE SOUTH PACIFIC by T.F.H. (Australia) Pty. Ltd., Box 149, Brookvale 2100 N.S.W., Australia; in NEW ZEALAND by Ross Haines & Son, Ltd., 18 Monmouth Street, Grey Lynn, Auckland 2, New Zealand; in the PHILIPPINES by Bio-Research, 5 Lippay Street, San Lorenzo Village, Makati Rizal; in SOUTH AFRICA by Multipet Pty. Ltd., 30 Turners Avenue, Durban 4001. Published by T.F.H. Publications, Inc. Manufactured in the United States of America by T.F.H. Publications, Inc.

CONTENTS

Why Choose a Cockatiel?...................................... 4

Selecting a Cockatiel 10

Taming a Cockatiel 20

Training a Cockatiel 34

Talking 48

Behavior Problems 56

Suggested Reading 63

Index................................64

WHY CHOOSE A COCKATIEL?

The Cockatiel is one of the most popular pet birds in the whole world, including its native Australia, where it must compete for attention with such exotic species as Cockatoos and Grass Parakeets. In fact, it's one of the top two pet parrots, second only to the ubiquitous and much less expensive Budgie. There are many good reasons why these petite yet charming birds continue to win new friends every day.

Cockatiels, known to scientists as *Nymphicus hollandicus*, evolved to live in the dry interior of the Australian continent, an environment which has shaped other pet quality birds such as the Zebra Finch and the Budgerigar. These birds are adapted to a nomadic existence, following the scarce rainfall from one region to another. Rather than aggressively defending an area against all comers, they tend to rely on a large flock of watchful eyes who can help spot water and watch out for predators across wide expanses of open territory. Hence, Cockatiels are innately sociable birds with a great need to interact with others. In captivity, that translates into a pet who looks forward to playing with its owner.

For the same reason, Cockatiels are much easier to keep and breed than tropical rain forest birds. Adapted to a semi-desert environment, they thrive on a seed-based diet that's far too protein-deficient for many other parrots. Furthermore, because the Australian rainy season is quite unpredictable, wild Cockatiels have to be ready to breed as soon as condi-

Opposite: The Cockatiel, like the Budgie, is a native of Australia. Wild Cockatiels are social birds that live in large flocks.

tions are right, instead of waiting for a special time. Hence, Cockatiels are relatively easy to breed in captivity, where there is always enough food and water, from the first. As a result, Cockatiels have been bred by humans for many generations—long enough for the birds to become domesticated.

Cockatiels became popular with the early parrot breeders for another reason: the adults are easy to sex. Many kinds of parrots, especially the larger ones, can't be sexed without an operation or some other specialized technique. As a result, breeders might pair two birds who were acting friendly and wait for years until they finally realized that they'd mated two girls or two boys. (Birds, with their strong social needs, can bond with members of their own sex or with members of other species if they don't have a proper mate. Their flexible nature is one reason why they can bond so strongly to a human being.) Consequently, people found breeding most parrots extremely frustrating. Adult Cockatiels, however, were easy to sex, so breeders could go to work on them right away.

So—which are the boys and which are the girls? With normal (gray) adults, it's easy to tell. After six months of age, the male will have a bright yellow face marked with a clear orange patch. The female has a duller face with varying amounts of gray, so that her orange patch doesn't stand out as brilliantly. She also retains the yellow bars on the underside of the tail that are present in juveniles of both sexes. A maturing male gradually loses these bars, replacing them with a dark gray, nearly black, coloring.

I highly recommend the Cockatiel if you've never trained a bird before—or even if you have. These amiable creatures are perfect for the beginner who might become buffaloed by the aggressive beak of a larger parrot. Naturally gentle and oriented toward a social existence, the pet Cockatiel lives for the chance to please a devoted owner. Furthermore, it's as easy to keep as any bird around, with a life expectancy of around 12 to 16 years. One famous Cockatiel lived to be 38, with the help of an extremely attentive owner and another bird who guided him around after he went blind in his old age.

In the wild, Cockatiels tend to look alike so that a predator can't pick out one bird and chase it to exhaustion. The

The normal plumage color of wild Cockatiels is gray; this coloration helps the birds blend into their surroundings.

normal, or gray variety, is the wild coloring because it helps the Cockatiel blend into its favorite perch, a dead tree. With the orange and yellow highlights on its face, the normal wild Cockatiel can look surprisingly like a gray branch with a spot of sunlight shining on it. Although many people, including me, find the natural bird an elegantly colored creature with a classic color scheme, other prospective Cockatiel owners may want to consider some of the different mutations that have been bred in captivity. The shade of a Cockatiel doesn't indicate anything about its trainability and personality, so you might as well choose the one you want, as long as the bird in question is young and healthy.

The most popular variety is probably the lutino, a Cockatiel that lacks black pigment and therefore has no black or gray on its feathers. As a result, the head feathers of both sexes are bright yellow with a clear orange patch. The body feathers can vary from a faint yellow wash to a brilliant sulfur

Profile of a pied Cockatiel. This color variety is also known as the harlequin, due to the patches of dark and light feathers.

yellow, and it is often the females who are the most vividly colored birds. Because it's a sex-linked mutation, the breeder can often tell you the sex of a lutino even though it isn't obvious to the eye. For instance, if two gray Cockatiels have a lutino baby, the breeder knows that the baby must be a female.

Unfortunately, many lutinos have a congenital bald spot on top of their heads. Don't buy the bird thinking the bald spot will grow over; it won't. Deep yellow lutinos are also prone to liver problems, so you must also be prepared to take special care with their diet.

The pied or harlequin is a variety that looks amusing rather than classically beautiful. These Cockatiels have white or yellow patches at irregular places over their bodies. No two pieds look exactly alike.

The pearly Cockatiel seemingly achieved its great popularity overnight. Each affected feather on these lovely birds is white or yellow with a dark gray border, giving the bird a rich scalloped look. At present, you can easily tell adult males from females because the males lose the pearly coloring during their first molt and thereafter look like normal grays. Some breeders, however, are currently working on programs to develop pearly males that retain their special plumage for a lifetime.

Lutino Cockatiel gnawing on a cuttlebone. Cuttlebone, available at pet shops, is a wonderful source of calcium for the pet parrot.

The true albino is a Cockatiel with no pigment, so that its feathers are snow white and its eyes are pink or red. You'll hear many people mistakenly refer to the lutino, which possesses yellow and red pigment, as an albino. However, the true albino is relatively expensive compared to the common Cockatiel varieties. You may also see a cinnamon, which is an attractive tan, or silver. The latter is a pale gray. The whiteface Cockatiel lacks red and yellow pigment, making it an elegant white and gray bird with no cheek patches. And, of course, you may encounter Cockatiels that sport a combination of colors, such as a Pied Pearly Whiteface. Whatever color you select, rest assured that you are making a wise choice in choosing a Cockatiel for your training project.

What do you want from your new Cockatiel? Because it's a living creature dependent on you for its care, you should never purchase a bird on a whim. Think carefully about your life style and expectations before you plunk down money for a Cockatiel.

SELECTING A COCKATIEL

What is your schedule like? Do you honestly have time to spend with your Cockatiel every day? Cockatiels are one of the easiest birds to tame and train, but even these good-natured animals can't tame themselves. If you work 80-hour weeks with scarcely enough time to catch the evening news or eat a hot meal, you are being unrealistic in expecting that you will have time to tame, much less play with, a pet bird.

Many busy people prefer to purchase two birds that can keep each other amused. Two Cockatiels in a suitable cage can usually find plenty to keep each other entertained, and yet they are unlikely to quarrel behind your back. However, I assume that you picked up a book on training Cockatiels because you want a bird that plays with you and performs for you. It's very difficult to convince a Cockatiel who already has a playmate that it must also learn to please you. As a general rule, you can't expect to completely tame a Cockatiel kept with others of its kind.

A Cockatiel must interact with others in order to stay healthy. It doesn't matter whether those others are Cockatiels or humans. The friend could even be a bird of another species that won't hurt the Cockatiel, such as a Budgerigar. What *does*

Opposite: Whatever color or sex Cockatiel you choose, be sure the plumage is clean and tight to the body.

matter is that the Cockatiel gets a chance to socialize with someone every day. If you want a beautifully tamed and trained Cockatiel who clamors for your attention, that someone should be you.

You should also ask yourself how important it is to you to have a talking bird. Cockatiels can learn to talk, but most do not. If you really want a talking bird but you have little money to spend, consider buying a young Budgerigar instead. These chatty little birds usually learn to talk much faster than Cockatiels, and they also tend to develop much larger vocabularies. Most Cockatiels, unless they are trained by extremely motivated owners, either don't talk or restrict their conversation to a few words or phrases.

If you have a problem with allergies, you may want to consult your doctor before buying a Cockatiel. Although birds aren't anywhere near as likely to cause problems as a fur-bearing animal like a dog or a cat, some people can be irritated by the fine white powder shed by Cockatiels and Cockatoos. In most cases, you'll be fine if you spray the Cockatiel with a light mist of pure water each day. However, if there is a strong possibility that you should be affected by this so-called "cockatoo dust," I suggest that you consider purchasing a Budgerigar instead.

All things considered, however, you'll probably find that the Cockatiel is one of the best choices around for taming and training. It's hardy, with an ability to survive on a relatively simple diet. It's gentle and easy to handle, with a beak that is far less intimidating than that of a larger parrot. And it's highly social throughout its life, meaning that it should remain an amiable pet for many years.

You won't have any trouble finding a wide selection of Cockatiels nearby. Both breeders and pet stores can regularly offer these prolific birds at reasonable prices. (However, if you decide to buy from a breeder, purchase the cage at a pet store or pet supply outlet before you bring the Cockatiel home. No bird should have to sit in a dark box while you dash around town shopping for a cage.) Take your time when you shop for your bird. Look around to see what various dealers have to offer. I wouldn't be overly concerned with price, since all Cocka-

Selecting a Cockatiel

Take great care when introducing your new Cockatiel to other pets, especially to larger animals such as dogs and cats.

tiels are quite inexpensive compared to other parrots of their size. I would be more interested in the overall condition of the store or aviary and the birds themselves rather than the chance to save ten or twenty dollars.

Start evaluating the seller the minute you walk in the door. Some parrots, such as Amazons, have a pronounced "birdy" scent, but a Cockatiel and its cage should *never* smell. If it does, choose another seller. A large aviary where Cockatiels are breeding may be somewhat dusty because the owner doesn't want to disturb the parent birds with a full cleaning, but a pet store where birds aren't being bred should be spotless. Wastes are going to accumulate on the bottom of a cage or a play stand over the course of the day, but feces shouldn't be caked on perches or collecting in the water dish. Use your judgment. The cleaner the shop, and the more caring the personnel, the more likely it is that you'll find healthy birds within.

While you're shopping, ask about the seller's guarantee. Many stores will offer to replace a bird who doesn't pass a health exam with a vet.

Since you're looking for a trainable Cockatiel, you should shop for the youngest bird you can get that's ready to leave the nest. Since it can be difficult or impossible to sex most sub-adult Cockatiels, that means you probably won't be able to choose the sex of your bird. Don't worry about it. Although there's lots of folklore on this subject, with some people claiming that males make better pets and others saying that it's the females who are more talented, the sex of the bird simply isn't anywhere near as important as its age when you start its training. To avoid confusion, it's a good idea to give your new Cockatiel a name that will be appropriate, no matter what sex it turns out to be.

How old is that Cockatiel? Is it young enough to make a good pet? Even if you're a rank beginner, you can make some pretty good guesses about the age of a juvenile Cockatiel.

A four-week-old Cockatiel. Cockatiels under the age of two months have pink beaks; once they are weaned, they make excellent candidates for taming.

A lutino Cockatiel. Young Cockatiels grow adult plumage at various ages; ask your pet dealer to help you determine the age of the bird in question.

These birds are already as long as the adults when they're ready to sell, but they're noticeably more slender when compared to an adult. Until they're about six months old, all of the juveniles will resemble females. With normal grays, that means that the young birds will be relatively dull, with heavy barring on the underside of the tail. Youngsters also show pale stripes on their chests that aren't visible in older birds. Cockatiels less than two or three months old will have pink rather than gray beaks. Because Cockatiels change to their adult coloring at varying rates, some birds will retain their youthful plumage longer than others.

In general, however, you can expect a slim Cockatiel with pale chest bars and a heavily barred tail to be somewhere under six months old—fine for taming purposes. For the best and most easily tamed pet, hold out for a just-weaned baby with a pink beak.

Some sellers offer handfed Cockatiels, birds that don't have to be tamed because they were fed by humans from the time they were babies. (They still have to be trained to do special tricks, of course.) Although you will pay more for these birds because of the extra human labor involved, the cost for a handfed Cockatiel isn't really that much out of line with the bird's usual price. If you've never worked with a bird before, you may feel more confident if some of the chore has already been done for you. Since they have never learned to fear humans, handfed babies generally make the sweetest and most affectionate pets. If they were talked to by their breeder, they may even know how to say a few words. Keep in mind, however, that a handfed Cockatiel needs love, time, and attention to stay affectionate.

Before buying a bird, give it a careful visual check-up. Never buy a Cockatiel who is already physically or mentally ill; it shouldn't be asked to cope with the stress of adjusting to a new home. Furthermore, you risk bringing home a disease that your other pets could catch. Let the seller cure the bird before you buy. If the bird is being abused, contact a humane society. A seller shouldn't be rewarded with your dollars for offering sick birds.

Watch how the Cockatiel behaves when you approach its cage or playpen. If it hasn't been tamed or handfed, it should show some signs of nervousness when you approach its cage. If it is tame, it may actively move forward, trying to solicit your attention. Tame or untame, the Cockatiel should be alert, with a keen interest in its surroundings. A bird who won't move or respond is probably too sick to care.

How does the Cockatiel sit on its perch? If it's puffed up to keep warm or sitting on the floor, pass it by. Of course, many birds siesta during the afternoon, but you should expect a healthy Cockatiel to doze on its perch with one foot drawn up to its belly. It should certainly open its eyes when you start talking to it or moving in close.

Check the body openings for discharges. The eyes and nostrils should be clear of watery fluids. (If you have never looked closely at a Cockatiel before, you may be concerned by a flat piece of tissue called the nasal turbinate, which looks like skin plugging the back of the nostrils. However, this feature is normal in Cockatiels.) When the seller captures the bird you want, turn it over to make sure that there are no caked feces blocking the vent. Reject any Cockatiel that has a suspicious discharge anywhere. The "sniffles" can be a serious medical problem in a bird.

An array of Cockatiels will be available at your local pet shop. Keep in mind that pet shops cannot possibly provide individual cages for every bird.

Feel the keelbone, the long bone running down the Cockatiel's chest that helps it fly. Young Cockatiels are slender, but they shouldn't be skinny. If the keelbone feels like a sharp knife sticking out of the flesh, the Cockatiel is too thin to withstand the stress of moving to a new home. Choose another bird.

Check the condition of the plumage. Rambunctious young birds may lose a tail feather or two in the usual rough and tumble of a dealer's playpen or community cage. Since the feathers grow back so quickly, that's no reason to reject a bird. However, don't buy a Cockatiel that has been picked to bits by itself or its companions. Any bird healthy enough for a taming project will have the self-respect to keep its feathers neat and clean. You should also remember that an otherwise perfectly

Be sure to check the head, body, and plumage of any bird you plan to buy.

beautiful lutino may have a bald spot on its head. If baldness bothers you or if you think you might ever want to breed the bird, make sure to check the head of each lutino you plan to buy.

Check the feet and toes. If there are bright red spots on the bottom of the foot, reject the Cockatiel. If a toe is missing but the bird seems otherwise healthy, you may be able to ask for a reduced price. Make sure that the toe has healed over cleanly before you agree to buy. A Cockatiel who can't perch comfortably because of foot problems certainly won't be able to focus its attention on its training.

Before you take your new Cockatiel home, ask the seller to clip its wings. Don't decide against wing-clipping out of a mistaken sense of concern for the bird. Wing-clipping doesn't hurt the bird any more than trimming your hair hurts you. What can hurt or even kill the Cockatiel is being fully flighted inside a house, where it can become startled and fly into a wall so hard that it breaks its neck. A new Cockatiel is in the most danger, since it doesn't know you yet and is more likely to become frightened. Even if you don't accidentally injure the free-flying bird, you will probably become quite frustrated in your attempts to tame the new pet. A flighted Cockatiel can be almost impossible to tame.

It isn't hard to clip a bird's wings. You will probably learn how sooner or later so that you can keep your pet's wings in trim. However, I strongly suggest that you have a person such as the seller or a professional groomer clip the Cockatiel's wings until it's tame enough to let you clip without a struggle. Some Cockatiels do hold grudges, so you'd be getting your relationship off to a bad start if you tried to clip the wings for the first time yourself.

The seller may offer to clip one or both wings. I prefer to clip one wing, so that the Cockatiel goes in circles when it tries to fly. That way, it quickly learns that it can't escape in the direction it's pointed at when it tries to fly. When both wings are clipped, some parrots can still fly amazingly well because they can still get some well-balanced lift on each wing.

For best results, choose *one* Cockatiel that's young, healthy, and alert. If you concentrate on one bird that's ready to learn, you should have no trouble turning your Cockatiel into a lovable pet.

Your local pet shop will have a variety of products especially designed for Cockatiels. It is a good idea to purchase necessities before bringing the bird home.

TAMING A COCKATIEL

Cockatiels are hardy birds, but they need time to get used to their new home. Be patient when you introduce the bird to its new family.

Get off on the right foot. Have a cage of the proper size situated in a quiet place that's free of drafts, strong odors, and temperature changes. Never keep a Cockatiel in the kitchen, where all three of these disturbing elements occur. Later, you will be able to move your Cockatiel into a busy family room, but start it off in some out-of-the-way place where it can relax and observe the household goings-on without feeling constantly watched.

Talk to the bird in a soft, reassuring voice each time you approach its cage, but don't start taming your pet on its first day. Give it a full 24 hours to get used to its new home. Although it may not eat in front of you yet, expect to find some hulled seeds as evidence that it has fed. If the Cockatiel hasn't eaten after 24 hours, contact the seller without delay. A small bird can starve to death in a very short period of time.

Naturally, everyone is going to be excited about the new pet. Children, in particular, will gather round to watch the Cockatiel. Explain to them that these creatures are shy at first. Insist that they speak in quiet voices around the bird. Don't allow anyone to poke inside its cage or to watch the bird hour after hour. (This includes any pet cats!) The new Cockatiel needs time to get used to its surroundings.

If you have other birds, keep the newly acquired Cockatiel quarantined in a separate room for two weeks to thirty days after its purchase. You may also want to have the new ac-

Opposite: A newly purchased Cockatiel will be nervous when it is first brought home.

quisition examined by a vet. Most Cockatiels are healthy, but you don't want to risk exposing your other birds to a disease. To be doubly safe, always feed the newest bird last, and wash your hands before and after handling a bird. It shouldn't be hard to develop the habit, since Cockatiels often leave behind some of their fine white powder as a reminder to wash off when you're finished playing.

How long will it take to tame your Cockatiel? That depends on you and your bird. If you have a handfed Cockatiel, you may be able to run through the whole chapter with your new bird in a few minutes. If you have an older Cockatiel, you may spend the first week just teaching it to step on a stick on command. For the most part, I'm assuming that you will be working with a younger bird—which means you can expect to teach the bird to step on and off your hand and accept petting within just a few lessons that shouldn't take more than a week. A pink-beaked baby could be climbing around your shoulders within 20 minutes.

Some pet shops will allow the new owner 24 hours in which to have the bird examined by a vet. Whether your pet shop has such a guarantee or not, taking the bird for a veterinary check-up is a good idea.

Some experts believe you should wait a few days after bringing the bird home before you begin training, while others believe you should start the next day.

You'll be pleasantly surprised at how easy it is to tame a Cockatiel, especially if you've chosen a just-weaned bird with a pink beak. Some experts advise waiting for several days or even a couple of weeks before beginning taming sessions with a new Cockatiel. I disagree. Cockatiels, like any other creature, learn most quickly when they're young and impressionable. The earlier you start taming the bird, the more quickly it will respond to its lessons. Once the bird has had a full 24 hours to relax and start eating, it's ready to begin.

Locate a safe, quiet spot to tame the new Cockatiel. The job will be a lot easier if the place you choose is all or partially enclosed, like a shower stall or a small room. Never try to tame a parrot in a room filled with knickknacks, heavy furniture, or lots of boxes. Otherwise, you will spend more time hunting down the Cockatiel or grabbing for delicate bric-a-brac than you will taming the bird.

A shower stall, especially one that can be closed with glass doors instead of curtains, is often ideal. However, make sure the whole bathroom is safe for the bird before you go to work. Put down the toilet lid, cover any mirrors with a soft towel, close the windows, and store away any chemicals. The strong-smelling chemicals that are often used for cleaning bathrooms can overwhelm a bird's delicate respiratory system, killing the bird, so don't bring a Cockatiel into the bathroom until every trace of chemical odor has vanished.

You must not allow any distractions when you're taming your Cockatiel. Turn off the radio, stereo, and TV. Remove any birds that are near the taming area, and ask any other people present to leave. Put cats, dogs, and other pets elsewhere for the duration. Take off all your jewelry, including your watch. (In fact, it's a good idea to remove jewelry any time you play with a parrot. Cockatiels may be small, but they have deft beaks. I've had a watch knob and a silver necklace cheerfully destroyed by Cockatiels.) Don't wear red, including bright red nail polish. Remove all toys from its cage. By the way, never give a Cockatiel a mirror until it's tamed and trained to your satisfaction. Otherwise, it may be too interested in attracting the bird it sees in the mirror to pay any attention to you.

If your Cockatiel is a young one in top notch condition, you can tame it in fairly short order by subjecting it to continuous contact that it can't escape. After a while, the Cockatiel's nervous system will become overwhelmed by your constant presence, causing it to stop trying to flee after a relatively short period. However, you'll understand that this technique puts quite a lot of stress on the Cockatiel. Since too much stress can weaken the bird's body, making it susceptible to disease, I strongly suggest that you reserve intensive training for young ones in perfect condition.

You will need to set aside several hours for the intensive training of your young Cockatiel. Bring the bird, cage and all, into the taming area, remembering to talk to the bird in a reassuring voice when you move it. You should also bring a perch, a cheap clock, and a supply of treats such as sunflower seeds or a sprig of millet spray. (If you withhold these treats from the regular feed cup, you're more likely to get the Cockatiel's interest in a hurry.) You might also wish to bring a book, so you can have something to read during the long intervals when you're simply letting the bird get used to having you around.

You may start work while the Cockatiel is still in its

cage. Sit by the cage for awhile, reading your book or just thinking your thoughts, giving the Cockatiel time to look you over. After a few minutes, slowly bring your hand close to the cage, offering the treat between two fingers. (Note: This trick can be hazardous with other species of parrots, many of whom are fiercely territorial and will bite if you stick your fingers in or around the cage.) Speak to the Cockatiel in a calm, soft voice,

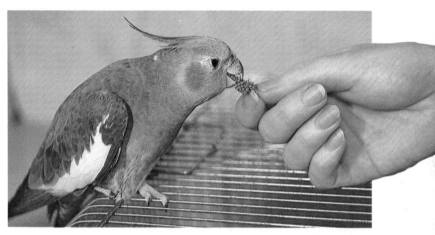

One of the first steps in taming the Cockatiel is getting the bird to accept a treat from your fingers while it is still in the cage.

telling it how pretty it is and how much you want to be its friend. Try to approach the bird from the side, where it can see you clearly with one eye. A predator would try to sneak up quietly on the Cockatiel from a rear or head-on position, so your actions communicate your good intentions to the bird.

If the Cockatiel is untame, it will try to frighten you away with a gesture of aggression. It may hiss like a snake, slash forward as if to bite you, or turn upside down and violently flap its wings. Don't be bluffed. Calmly pause for a moment, holding your hand where it is. Wait until the bird has quieted some before you start moving forward again. Whatever you do, however, don't jerk your hand back. You don't want a three-ounce Cockatiel to think it has you running scared, do you?

If you move forward slowly, talking softly, you will eventually get to the point where you can stick the treat in the cage. Be patient. Sooner or later, probably sooner, the Cockatiel will grab for the treat. Praise it in a soft but happy voice. Don't be afraid to let your pleasure show. Not all Cockatiels will eat the treat, but continue to praise them whether they're munching away or flinging the food to the floor of the cage.

Don't try to tame the Cockatiel for more than 20 minutes at a time. Birds have a short attention span, and they need time to consider what they've learned. If 20 minutes have already passed, return to your book. Let the bird watch you for the next hour or so as you relax. Then you can move on to the next step.

Open the cage door. Holding a treat between two fingers, move your hand into the cage. Talk softly and continuously. Again, if the Cockatiel fusses, freeze your hand in place

Some owners try to have the Cockatiel step on their fingers right away, while others prefer to start with a wooden perch.

for a few moments, but don't pull back. Move closer and closer to the bird, gradually raising your hand to the level of its chest. Once you get to that point, the Cockatiel is almost guaranteed to step onto your hand because it, like all parrots, feels safest when it's sitting on the highest perch. Don't jerk back your hand when the Cockatiel uses its beak as a steadying third leg to step onto your hand. It isn't going to bite you when it does that. However, if it's still slashing and hissing like it intends to bite, stop moving your hand forward until the bird is calm.

If your pet becomes nervous and flies up to your shoulder or head, remain calm and try to get it down with your finger or a wooden stick.

If you have a great fear of being bitten, you can start the taming sessions by using a perch instead of your hand. However, if the Cockatiel is really frightened, hissing and spitting for an inordinate amount of time, you should change your training technique to the less stressful gradual method.

Once the Cockatiel is on your hand, slowly try to move it out of the cage. Keep sweet-talking it. Pause each time the bird gets nervous or steps off. Remember to take a long break after 15 or 20 minutes, but don't be tied to the clock. Try to end each session on a high note. If the Cockatiel is already riding your hand by the end of ten minutes, place it on top of its cage for a rest.

Taming a Cockatiel

Once outside of the cage, the Cockatiel may panic and try to fly. Wait until it lands, and calmly pick it up with your hand or the stick. Remember to move your hand (or stick) in from the side at chest level, so that the bird will step onto it naturally. The Cockatiel will want to fly off several times to test its wings, so be patient. And keep up the smooth talk! Praise the bird effusively each time it steps on your hand or accepts a treat from your fingers.

Is it time for a break yet? When the Cockatiel's had a rest, try a game called ladder. While it's standing on one hand, slowly approach it with the other and invite it to step up. When it does, move the other hand in to get it to step up again. Continue until both hands are stretched out over your head.

Now you need to teach the Cockatiel to step off your hand. It may be hard to believe, but once it's tame, you'll have a lot more trouble putting it into the cage than getting it out. Slowly move the Cockatiel so that the roof of its cage is at its chest level. It should automatically step off. You can also practice actually placing the Cockatiel back inside its cage, placing the cage perch at chest level so that it can step off onto that.

Your Cockatiel is technically tame when it's no longer afraid of humans, and steps on and off your hand on command. Congratulations! If you have a pink-beaked baby, you may well have tamed your Cockatiel within an hour. However, be patient and take the time to schedule plenty of breaks if you haven't. Each Cockatiel is an individual, so I can't predict exactly how long it will take to tame the bird—but it should certainly be faster and easier than, say, housebreaking a new puppy!

What if the Cockatiel bites you or does something else undesirable, such as landing on your head? Be calm, reminding yourself that a Cockatiel can't do real damage. (It's possible for a Cockatiel to bite hard enough to draw blood, but it's unlikely.) Never hit the bird. Birds learn nothing from physical punishment except fear, which will make the animal much harder to

Opposite: "Ladder" is a favorite game with pet Cockatiels. You can use your fingers, wooden dowels, or both.

If your Cockatiel bites you, tell the bird "No" in a loud voice. Never hit your pet for biting.

tame. What you should do is tell the bird, "No!" in a loud, clear voice whenever it bites or lands on your head. Then return immediately, but calmly, to the lesson at hand.

Cockatiels aren't big on being cuddled the way some Cockatoos are. However, you will be doing both of you a big favor if you teach your bird to accept being petted and handled all over its body. Nail-trimming, wing-clipping, and veterinarian exams are all infinitely more pleasant when the Cockatiel in question has learned that you mean it no harm when you pick it up.

I start by scratching the Cockatiel's cheek patches. Move in very slowly from the side, talking all the while. Many Cockatiels are initially disturbed when you approach their head, so be prepared to wait out a hiss-and-spit session before you reach your goal. Once you're actually scratching gently around the Cockatiel's ears, you'll be amazed by its change in attitude. It may peep delightedly, bumping its head against your hand to urge you on each time you stop. Then you may get hissed at when you have to stop scratching the Cockatiel to attend to your other duties!

You may want to spend a couple of weeks or more on head-scratching before you start to move your hand over the bird's back. Cockatiels dislike this position because it reminds them of being grabbed by a predator, so be very patient. Gradually work yourself into a position where you can close your hands over the wings. You can pick up the bird from this position if you encircle the wings so it can't flap and hurt itself, but don't put any pressure on the chest. Keep a finger on either side of the bird's head to hold it where it can't bite you.

Again, you may want to develop your relationship with your Cockatiel a little further before you attempt to pick it up or cuddle it from the back. However, you shouldn't delay forever. The Cockatiel may dislike all-over body cuddling, but its resigned acceptance of the treatment could save its life if it should get sick or become injured.

Let's turn to the gradual method of taming your Cockatiel. Perhaps you don't have several hours in one clump to work on the project, or maybe you would prefer to reduce the stress on the bird. You may have an older adolescent, perhaps one that was raised in an aviary and thus totally unaccustomed to human handling. Perhaps your friends, impressed by the tameness of your pet Cockatiel, have asked you to train the adult bird they never got around to.

It will take a lot of patience to tame a fully adult Cockatiel. If your friends are really that busy, they might do better to pair the bird off with another of its own kind. In the other cases, however, you should do just fine taming the bird at a slower pace. You will be teaching the Cockatiel the same things you would if you were taming it in a single intensive session— leaving its cage, riding a hand and a stick, accepting a head-scratch. However, you should make sure that each lesson lasts no longer than 20 to 30 minutes at a time. Between lessons, which should be at least an hour or more apart, leave the bird alone to recover. If the Cockatiel is really nervous, it won't eat or relax until you're gone, so these breaks are very important.

You must use a lot more patience with an older bird. You can't expect it to be running up and down your shoulders after only an hour, the way a handfed bird might. Take your time, offer treats, and praise it effusively. Never, ever lose your temper, even if the bird tries to bite you. Tell it, "No," as loudly as you wish, and move onto something positive. The Cockatiel will need more time to learn to trust you if it has never been close to humans before, but it will learn. Be patient, and keep working with the bird every day until it can do everything in this chapter.

Patience, praise, and more patience are the key words in training a pet Cockatiel.

Always keep in mind that a Cockatiel's attention span is quite short. Don't overdo it!

Up to this point, one person has been in charge of taming the Cockatiel. Now, however, it's time to try the Cockatiel with other people. Ask the new person to move slowly, talking softly. He or she should hold a hand up to the bird's chest, inviting it to climb aboard. If the Cockatiel goes willingly, you're in luck. The Cockatiel is completely tame! If not, ask the second person to use patience in winning over the bird. Within a short time, the Cockatiel should learn to enjoy anyone who's in and out of the house on a regular basis. Remember to ask visitors to remove their jewelry. A tame Cockatiel has just as much fun destroying a pair of diamond earrings as an untame one would, probably more.

You will successfully tame your Cockatiel if you remember the following points: 1) Several short sessions of less than 20 minutes are better than one long session of an hour or more; 2) Always keep talking in a reassuring voice; and 3) Be patient. The days or weeks you spend in taming the bird are an investment that ensures that the months and years ahead are rewarding for both you and your Cockatiel.

TRAINING
A COCKATIEL

Once you've tamed your new Cockatiel, you will want to train your pet to perform tricks and to play with you. That's great! Training, undertaken correctly, enhances your relationship with your Cockatiel in a number of ways.

In the wild, a Cockatiel would spend a lot of time ranging over open territory, hunting for food and water while avoiding predators. In captivity, the bird needs something else to exercise its active body and mind. By giving the Cockatiel something challenging to do, you keep its intellect sharp and its body in tune. A bird who is excited about life and interested in its environment is almost always healthier than a bored, depressed bird. Zoo keepers have long reported that performing birds routinely outlive untame ones.

A trained Cockatiel is more fun for most people to be around. Because the bird can get your attention in positive ways, it's less likely to resort to monotonous peeping or threat displays to tell you it's ready to play. Furthermore, it's a fact of human nature that most people will tend to spend more time playing with a well-trained bird. Both you and the Cockatiel will be happier as a result of a good training program.

Although it's possible to train a completely wild animal—ask any lion tamer!—virtually all home training takes place *after* the bird is already tame. Any training session is a lot more fun if both you and the Cockatiel are relaxed. Take all the time you need with the previous chapter, patiently ensuring that your Cockatiel feels safe and happy around you. When it starts bopping its head against your hand to get you to scratch its cheek patches, you're on your way.

Opposite: The Cockatiel is an intelligent bird that can be taught any number of tricks.

You teach an animal tricks by conditioning it to react in the same, desired way each time you give a particular command. "Conditioning" simply means that you teach the animal to associate a particular activity with something it really likes, such as a favorite food. In time, you no longer have to offer the treat each time the bird performs the activity, because it has learned to do it automatically in response to the command.

You can train your Cockatiel using either food or affection rewards. In practice, most people use a combination of both. As you prepare to train your bird, watch to see if it has any favorite foods. Cockatiels tend to have narrow appetites, but many have a weakness for sunflower seeds or millet sprays. When you fill the Cockatiel's food dish each day, hold back the special foods to use as treats during your training sessions.

Some people don't like to interrupt the training to wait for the bird to eat its treat, so they offer only affection rewards. I find that affection training works just as well or better than offering food. (I have a Cockatiel who actually acts as if she's offended when I offer food instead of a shower mist or a cheek scratching!) A tame pet who really loves you has an incredible motivation to please. Lavish your petting and praise on your pet when it performs correctly. Don't worry about the Cockatiel developing a swelled head from all the attention. Everyone loves an avian "ham" who lives for the chance to perform for its beloved humans.

Never hurry when you're training a bird. Remember that your Cockatiel has a short attention span. Each lesson should last no more than 20 to 30 minutes. As when taming, try to end each lesson on a high point. If it takes the Cockatiel 15 minutes to learn half of a trick, praise it for what's accomplished, and go ahead and take a break. There are no prizes for "Fastest Trained Cockatiel."

All of the basic guidelines required for taming a Cockatiel hold true for training. Remove all distractions: other birds, people, mirrors, extra toys, jewelry. Turn off the TV, the stereo, and the radio. Find a safe, quiet spot for the lessons.

One of the most valuable lessons you can teach a Cockatiel is to "come" on command. This easy lesson will also familiarize you with the basics of training.

Once your Cockatiel has been tamed and has learned to enjoy your attention, trick training can begin.

Since the Cockatiel has clipped wings, place it somewhere that allows it to easily walk over to you. Then tell it to "Come" in a firm, pleasant voice. Since it's tame, it may well hurry over simply because it wants to be with you, not because you've given the command. Don't worry about its motives. Reward it with effusive praise and a treat. Tell it what a smart bird it is. Repeat the lesson several times in sessions that last no more than 20 minutes. If the Cockatiel doesn't come to you, repeat the command until it does. Never scold. Simply refuse to praise the bird until it does what you're asking. In a few lessons, it should be walking over to you each time you ask, unless it's distracted. (Remove the distraction!)

Now you can test the Cockatiel a little. Place it further away before you give the command to "come." Don't spare the praise when it obeys.

A fully flighted Cockatiel may lose some of its tameness; therefore, it is usually recommended that its wings be clipped periodically to prevent accidents and escape.

I should add a word of warning here. Once your Cockatiel comes when it's called, you may feel that it's safe to let its wings grow out. I wouldn't risk it. You never know when a loud noise or some other unforeseen incident could frighten the Cockatiel so badly that it forgets its lessons and sails out the door. (Once a neighbor's cat actually sneaked into my house!) Because they evolved from ground-feeding birds, Cockatiels have an instinct to fly up fast and hard. Before you know it, your precious pet could be tangled up in a ceiling fan or bouncing off a wall.

Many people also report that fully flighted Cockatiels, especially males, tend to lose some of their tameness. Because they can fly away, they may feel that the balance of power has changed in your relationship. Some birds seem to positively enjoy watching the baffled human huff and puff about the room as they gracefully glide away.

Most Cockatiels aren't housebroken, but you can certainly train your bird to defecate over its cage when you give the word. You have to be patient and highly motivated. Most potty training lessons don't go anywhere because the owner decides it's easier to clean away the Cockatiel's small, compact feces. Cockatiels are creatures of habit, so it isn't hard to paper the three or four favorite places that your pet visits on a regular basis. However, with a little more work, you can make sure that your pet seldom or never leaves a little green gift on your new shirt.

Choose a word or short phrase that you would never use in normal conversation to be the command for defecation. "Shazzam!" or "Go potty" are fine. (If you were to use a more common word, you might accidentally give the command while the Cockatiel's sitting on your shoulder.) You should also be aware that Cockatiels aren't built to "hold it," so you'll need to give it a chance to defecate in a safe place every 20 or 30 minutes.

Each time you begin to play with the Cockatiel, hold it over its cage or playpen for a few minutes, giving the com-

Before you begin a training session, be sure all distractions, such as other pets, are out of the room.

mand. When it goes, praise it heavily. Be patient. Once it has defecated, you can move on to something else. In 20 or 30 minutes, return the Cockatiel to the top of its cage and give the command again. When it defecates, reward it.

Potty training can take a lot of time and patience because you can't give more than one lesson every 30 minutes or so. However, it's certainly worth the work—especially if you have squeamish friends or lots of white clothes.

You can use the same basic principles to teach Cockatiels showier tricks. Try to work with the bird's natural gestures, especially at first. Unlike other parrots, most Cockatiels don't hold food in their claws, so they aren't the naturals at pulling toys that other parrots are. However, they can be trained to do many clever tricks that involve using their *beaks* as hands. Some easy tricks include walking up a ladder, ringing a bell, or riding a radio-controlled car.

Putting a penny in a bank is a good example of a fairly complicated trick that a Cockatiel can perform. You need to start by letting the Cockatiel get used to the prop, a colorful piggy bank with a fairly wide slot. (Make sure that the toy is safe for a "chewy" bird. If it's made in the U.S. for a small child, the paint will be nontoxic, but some imported ceramics contain dangerous amounts of lead.) I wouldn't use an all-red piggy bank, although a little red detailing around the coin slot might be just the thing to attract the Cockatiel to the right place. You might want to place the piggy bank near the bird's cage or playpen for several hours or days to give the Cockatiel a chance to look it over. Not all Cockatiels are afraid of new toys, but many are.

Once the Cockatiel is no longer afraid of the piggy bank, you can start your lessons. Use a bright, shiny penny. (You can make sure it's clean by dropping it in boiling water. Let it cool completely before giving it to the Cockatiel.) Pennies manufactured after 1982 are not pure copper, so they tend to stay shinier than the real thing. Parrots love glitter, and starting with a brighter coin insures that you'll capture the bird's interest.

Ask the Cockatiel to pick up the coin. Repeat the words clearly and firmly. When it picks up that fascinating shiny object, praise it to the skies. Now tell the Cockatiel to drop the coin in the bank. Since it won't understand what you want at first, you will probably be lucky if it takes a few steps before dropping the coin on the floor. That's OK. Praise it for taking those steps.

Time and patience are just as essential in trick training as they are during the taming procedure.

As lessons progress, expect the bird to pick up the coin without praise. Lavish your good words on it only when it carries the coin in the right direction. As it approaches the bank, you can tap your fingers near the slot to draw its attention to the right place. When at last it drops the penny in the slot, reward it well. In succeeding lessons, reward the bird only when it shows improvement. Be patient, and never make the Cockatiel work on a lesson so long that it gets tired and grouchy. With time and patience, you should have the Cockatiel picking up the coin and dropping it into the slot without hesitation as soon as you give the command.

Now that you know the basics of trick training, you are ready to design your own tricks. As I mentioned with the piggy bank, you need to be careful in choosing your props. Let's look at some toys that can help you develop your Cockatiel's potential safely and easily.

Despite the fact that a Cockatiel may allow itself to be gently bossed by a small Budgerigar, the Cockatiel is a substantially stronger bird. Many bird toys that are fine for Budgies are much too flimsy for Cockatiels. The larger bird could actually hurt itself by swallowing a plastic bead or chewing open a toy penguin to munch on the lead weight inside. The best toys are usually found in shops that specialize in birds. Here the staff can help you choose a toy that's safe and inviting for a Cockatiel.

If you check the pet bird magazines or attend bird shows, you can also find specialists who sell more ambitious

Cockatiel playpens, available at pet shops, provide a wealth of training opportunities. All you need is patience and a little imagination.

toys for birds like bird-sized bicycles, roller skates, and merry-go-rounds. Designed by bird fanciers, these sturdy toys can make great props for impressive tricks. However, many of the props are designed for larger birds. Look for the toys that are sized for small conures and Cockatiels. You can also check regular toy stores. Since human youngsters also explore their world by putting things in their mouths, toys made for children under three are designed to be nontoxic if chewed. Anything that a conure or a toddler can enjoy but not destroy should be fine for a Cockatiel.

Let your Cockatiel enjoy toys from the very beginning. The younger you start, the better. It's usually the older birds who weren't handled by humans until they were six months old or even older who show a fear of toys. With these Cockatiels, you must use infinitely more patience in training the bird. You will probably have to spend several sessions just picking up the Cockatiel and placing it near or on the toy. If a Cockatiel really fears a toy, you might want to place it near the cage for a few days so that the bird can look it over on its own time.

Red, as I've mentioned before, is a powerful attention-getter. A Cockatiel may learn to chew a red rawhide doughnut in record time. However, some parrots show definite fear or aggression around red toys. Wait until your Cockatiel is tame and trustworthy before introducing this color.

Watch out for mirrors! If the Cockatiel can see its reflection in a shiny toy, it may fall in love with that splendid bird—and then you could be left out in the cold.

For the most playful Cockatiel, give the bird a playpen as well as a cage. In general, your Cockatiel will view the cage as a personal retreat where it can rest, eat, drink, and generally goof off, enjoying some private time where it's in control of the activities. An open playpen gives it a place where it can interact with its humans and show off its tricks. It also gets the Cockatiel off your shoulder to a safe place where you can actually see the bird without twisting your neck around like an owl.

You can build or buy a nice playpen for Cockatiels without too great an investment. Sure, the Cockatiel will eventually practice some serious chewing on that tempting white pine or birch. That's OK. Cockatiels, like any other parrots, need to chew to keep their beaks in trim. With a few basic tools and some clean dowels or wood scraps, you can easily keep your Cockatiel's playpen full of things to do. You can string blocks of wood on sturdy chains, create ladders and swings, and whittle an assortment of nice branches.

One warning: be careful to choose nontoxic woods that are safe for birds such as pine, birch, and cactus wood. You can use green branches from willow, fruit trees, and privet if you are sure that the tree in question hasn't been sprayed for several years. (That lets out most mature fruit-bearing trees, unfortunately.) An insecticide is a poison which can harm or kill a small bird.

If you give your Cockatiel a safe place to indulge its natural curiosity, you can reward it for exploring its environment without putting it in danger. Praise it when it plays with its toys. Let it enjoy a special treat while it's on the playpen. That way, you could have the Cockatiel climbing ladders and ringing bells on its own, with little or no work from you.

Of course, a *trained* Cockatiel will ring the bell or climb the ladder on command. Choose a different command for each activity and use it consistently. You can start by saying the phrase each time the bird starts to do the activity. When the bird performs, pile on the praise. With time, the Cockatiel will learn to associate the activity with the right words.

To a large extent, a Cockatiel's "talent" is a reflection of two things: the age at which it was trained and the dedication of its trainer. Once the bird has learned to learn, it can pick up new tricks all its life. However, most Cockatiels will reach a plateau period, after which they will learn few or no more tricks. Usually, this plateau coincides with the place where the owner got busy with something else and stopped training the bird. Keep working with your Cockatiel and you may be amazed by its high intelligence and sense of play.

Most people want to show off their Cockatiels to their friends. That's fine. Start slowly, having the Cockatiel perform when only one or two other people are present. Make sure the bird can do its tricks in front of the whole family without getting distracted. At all times, remember the attention span of the creature. A child might be capable of watching a Cockatiel

Keep in mind that an adult Cockatiel that has not had prior experience will usually be much more difficult to train than a youngster.

perform for hours, but the bird really needs its regular breaks to keep from getting grouchy and resentful. Trick time should be fun for everybody, including the Cockatiel.

Again, the sooner you start, the better. A three-month-old Cockatiel who isn't set in its ways will accept a crowd much better than an older bird who may have been poked at for months in a pet shop. Make sure that everyone who wants to handle the bird knows how to do so. Children, in particular, need to be watched to make sure they don't accidentally squeeze the Cockatiel through its abdomen. Never push the Cockatiel off on anyone who is afraid of birds.

Maybe your Cockatiel is such a ham that you're thinking of taking it to perform at a bird show, a charity fund-raiser, or a neighborhood fair. I would ask you to think very carefully before taking such a step. There is always the chance that a bird will be frightened, lost, or stolen during a trip outside its home, especially if it will be performing out-of-doors. Always check the Cockatiel's wings before you take it anywhere, trimming any feathers that have grown back so it can't fly too far away if it's startled.

If you belong to a bird club, why not plan some time at each meeting where performing birds could come out for practice? Each member with a trained bird would get a chance to see how it behaves in front of a crowd. As a side benefit, you could actually increase attendance at club meetings, since everyone enjoys watching birds perform. In any event, I wouldn't ask my Cockatiel to perform in public until I'd had a chance to see how it did in a low-pressure situation. Make sure it enjoys being around a roomful of strange people before you ask it to hang upside down from its toenails while ringing a bell. It's natural to want to show off your clever Cockatiel. However, you would probably never stop kicking yourself if the bird was frightened into having an accident or fleeing the room just because you wanted to prove to your friends that the bird really does all you said.

There are no secrets to training a Cockatiel. With patience, love, and an understanding of your bird's needs, you should be able to shape your pet into a performer that you'll be proud of.

Opposite: Your trick training attempts will be more successful if you try to work within the Cockatiel's sphere of innate behaviors, such as climbing and using the beak.

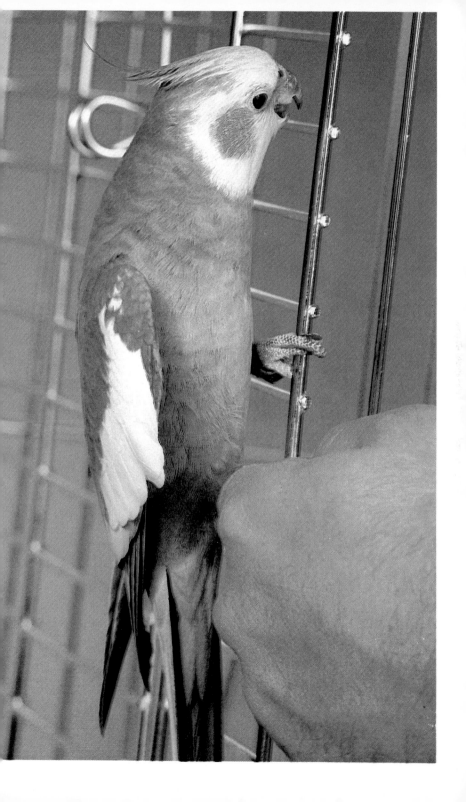

TALKING

Don't make your love for your Cockatiel contingent on its ability to talk. The vast majority of pet Cockatiels never learn how to talk, and even the talkers are rarely as gifted as many other parrot species. In a survey reported by *Bird Talk* magazine, only one out of 52 Cockatiels had a vocabulary of more than 100 words. By contrast, two out of six ringnecked parakeets had a vocabulary of more than 100 words. The average Cockatiel who did know how to talk used only 19 words, while the average ringneck knew 77 words.

Both male and female Cockatiels can learn how to talk. However, many people feel that males, who tend to be noisier and hence more vocal, make the best talkers. Of course, this generalization won't help too much since you will buy a Cockatiel before it's old enough to show its sex. I wouldn't worry about it. You certainly shouldn't wait to see what sex the bird is before you start lessons. Whether your pet is male or female, it will have a much better chance of learning to talk if you start the lessons as soon as possible.

You need a great deal of patience to teach a Cockatiel to talk, and you may not see any results for several months. It's possible for a Cockatiel to learn to talk from day-to-day conversation, but it's unlikely. You're going to have to work for real results.

Cockatiels tend to have clear, high-pitched voices. It may be easier for them to imitate the voice of a woman or a child, rather than a man. If several people are vying for the chance to teach the Cockatiel to talk, you might want to choose

Opposite: Keep in mind that the Cockatiel is not the most loquacious member of the parrot family—every word or song your pet learns must be amply rewarded.

the one with the highest-pitched voice. Whoever takes on the job, however, should be aware that it could take weeks or months.

Schedule a minimum of two 15-minute sessions each day. Mornings before work and evenings when you get home are fine. Place the Cockatiel on your hand or finger and repeat the first word you want it to learn. For some reason, "Hello" can be a hard word for parrots to pronounce. I would recommend that you start with a short phrase or the bird's name. "Pretty bird," which contains p's and r's, is relatively easy for most parrots to start off with.

Repeat the word or phrase in a clear, firm tone. Pause between each phrase. At first the Cockatiel may just look at you like you're nuts. That's where patient consistency comes in. The room where you're training the Cockatiel must be quiet, with all distractions removed. The bird must have nothing to think about except the words you're saying.

In time, the Cockatiel may actually start "peeping" as if it's trying to repeat the word. That's great. However, it may also remain quiet during the lessons, yet practice on its own when it's in its cage or on its playpen. Listen to its vocalizations. When it starts trying to modulate its peeps into words, you will know that you're on your way.

You can use the wonders of the electronic age to help you teach your Cockatiel to talk. Mail order companies and pet shops sell recordings of popular phrases like, "Pretty bird," and "I can talk. Can you fly?" Some companies even offer videos that you can show on TV so that the Cockatiel can see another bird repeating the words! My birds seem to prefer music videos to programs with other birds, but it could be worth a try. My favorite device is a blank endless loop cassette. I can record whatever phrase I want and let it play for however long I happen to be out of the room.

Of course, the Cockatiel will "tune out" a monotonous phrase if you aren't careful. Don't overplay your tape. It's tempting to leave the cassette on the whole time you're at work, but all that will do is teach the Cockatiel to ignore the irritating phrase. You should also make sure the bird isn't being distracted by the radio or toys. A good time to play the tape is

Listen closely when your Cockatiel starts to vocalize—it may be practicing the word you're trying to teach.

first thing in the morning while the Cockatiel's cage is still covered and last thing at night right after you've covered it for the evening. Since the Cockatiel is relaxed, with nothing else to concentrate on, it can devote its entire attention to the new words.

Be careful! Once I trained a parrot by playing a tape each morning while I took my shower. As a result, the bird tried to talk only when it heard running water. Take care to prevent the Cockatiel from forming false associations.

I wish I could tell you that you could turn over the whole chore to your VCR or cassette recorder. Alas, it isn't true. The electronic marvels work, but they are no substitute for the human touch. You must continue to schedule at least one, and preferably two, 15-minute training sessions for your Cockatiel each day. It may be possible for a Cockatiel to learn to talk from machines alone, but what good would that do?

Always speak slowly and clearly to your pet; in addition, try to choose simple words that are easy for the bird to pronounce.

You want the bird to talk to please you, not to amuse itself when you're miles away.

You must monitor your language around any bird that's learning to talk. Perhaps because certain words are spoken explosively, in moments of frustration, they can really capture the imagination of a talking bird. You have been warned.

Some people think that it's "cute" to teach taboo

words to a sweet-natured bird like the Cockatiel. I can't agree. Think about how the bird will feel if it must be hidden away from family and friends because of its language. It won't understand what it did to get banished from the center of things. Perhaps it will decide not to talk at all. Perhaps it will become depressed and anxious.

If a Cockatiel picks up an objectionable word, don't scold it. The bird may decide that it's talking you don't like, not the word. The best thing to do is to totally ignore the Cockatiel when it says the taboo word. Since it's talking to win your love and attention, it should eventually drop a word that gets neither.

Many birds won't talk in front of strangers, especially at first. That can be embarrassing, especially since the first thing most people ask about a Cockatiel is, "Can it talk?" Understand that a bird talks in order to draw the attention of the people it loves. The Cockatiel that calls your name when it wants attention may clam up when it sees your friend, simply because it isn't sure that it wants this stranger to notice it. Just as you did when you were taming and training the bird, take your time about introducing it to new people. Make sure it's comfortable and chatty around everyone in the family before you try the Cockatiel on outsiders.

You can also train your Cockatiel to repeat appropriate phrases in response to short questions or actions. If the bird says, "Hello," for instance, greet the bird with a "Hello" each time you come home. Praise the bird when it answers you with its own "Hello." If it says something else, simply ignore it until it hits upon the right answer. Once you have taught the Cockatiel to respond automatically, you will find it much easier to get it to talk around strangers.

Many birds won't talk in a perfectly quiet house. In the wild, a bird would go silent when everybody else did, because it would assume that somebody spotted a predator. Your Cockatiel has the same instincts. If everyone is stone quiet, staring intently at the bird, it may go on the alert and stay silent. If you carry on with your own conversation, paying attention to the Cockatiel when it's appropriate, you will soon convince the bird that it's safe to talk.

Your Cockatiel will learn as many words as you teach it. Many people get exhausted by the effort of teaching their Cockatiels one word or phrase, giving up as soon as they've reached that goal. But you shouldn't quit now! Once the Cockatiel has gotten the idea of talking, it can learn new words and phrases much faster. Spend time rehearsing the word with your Cockatiel each day, and play its cassette on a regular basis. You may be surprised at your bird's gift for chatter.

Whistling is more natural to a Cockatiel than talking, so you might want to consider teaching your pet to whistle a short tune. Teach it one line at a time, waiting until it has perfected one line before moving onto the next. Again, personal lessons are best. However, if no one in the family can whistle, go ahead and try using pre-recorded tapes. A vocal Cockatiel, especially a male, may pick up the tune simply from hearing the tapes. Think about what you're doing before you do it, however. Many people are sorry that they taught their parrots to wolf whistle, since it's a loud penetrating sound that pretty much stops all conversation in the room. You would be wise to pick a pleasant, popular tune, such as "Yankee Doodle" or "Pop Goes the Weasel" instead.

Opposite: It is possible for your Cockatiel to learn a few words and a few simple melodies. Keep in mind that your pet's endeavors should always be suitably praised and appreciated.

BEHAVIOR PROBLEMS

It's always easier to prevent a behavior problem than to deal with it once it has appeared. Many Cockatiels become problem birds due to unintentional neglect. Don't forget your pet when you're busy or under stress. Your Cockatiel wants and needs love and attention, whether from another bird or from you. If it can't get your attention in a positive way, it may resort to negative attention-getters like shrieking or feather plucking. If you can force yourself to slow down and enjoy your pet, both of you will be happier and more relaxed.

If your Cockatiel seems to "go wild" once it has matured, check its wings. As I mentioned earlier, some Cockatiels lose some tameness when their wings grow out. You can easily head off this problem by keeping your pet's wings neatly trimmed. Although you will probably take your Cockatiel to the pet groomer for the first couple of times, you will eventually want to learn how to do this chore for yourself. It really isn't difficult, and you're unlikely to make a serious mistake. Even if you do an uneven job at first, relax. The feathers will always grow out.

Assemble your supplies before you start. You will need a soft, dry towel, a pair of good scissors, and some styptic powder on the off chance that you hit a blood feather. If the Cockatiel is very tame, it may allow you to hold out its wing for a quick clipping. If not, have a partner hold the bird in the towel. Flip some of the cloth over the Cockatiel's head so that it can't see what's going on. It should fall quiet in the darkness; in fact, many birds start to chew contentedly on the towel. The person holding the Cockatiel should take care never to press hard on the bird's abdomen, which could interrupt its breathing.

Clip *only* the long outer feathers on the end of the wing to prevent hitting a still-growing blood feather. Again, you have the choice of clipping one wing or both. If you clip only one wing, the bird may be able to get into the air but it won't be able to control the direction of flight. If you clip both wings, the bird may not be able to fly at all—at least until some of the feathers return. In either case, check the length of the

Many aviculturists advocate clipping only one of the bird's wings. That way, the bird cannot control the direction of its flight and is less likely to attempt a dangerous escape.

Cockatiel's wing feathers on a regular basis. You may need to trim the bird from two to four times a year at regular intervals to prevent it from regaining its power of flight.

If the Cockatiel stays sweet when it grows back its feathers, you may choose to let it stay fully flighted. If so, be aware that your choice carries a serious responsibility. Make sure all doors and windows leading outside are closed *and* locked whenever the bird is outside of its cage. No matter how well-trained is your Cockatiel, it could easily panic or become confused once it has escaped out-of-doors. In the excitement of exploring its new world, it may not realize that it doesn't know how to find its way home until it's too late.

Sooner or later, you will also have to clip the Cockatiel's nails. Again, watch a pro do the job for the first couple of times. When you're ready to try it yourself, get a towel, a pair of puppy toenail clippers, a nail file, and styptic powder. While your partner holds the Cockatiel in the towel, quickly clip or file the very end of the bird's nails. It's better to take off too little and have to repeat the job in a week or so than to take too much. However, don't panic if you accidentally draw blood. Quickly press some styptic powder onto the injured toe, applying direct pressure. The bleeding should stop almost immediately. You will have an easier time avoiding injury with pale-footed Cockatiels, since you will be able to avoid the vein. Shine a strong light through the bird's foot, and you should see the dark outline of the vein running through the nail.

Some people complain that their Cockatiels peep monotonously for hour after hour. If the bird is fussing at an impossible time, the best thing to do is to cover the cage for 15 or 20 minutes. Most birds instinctively fall silent in total darkness because they don't want to attract the attention of a predator that they can't see.

However, if there is a lot of noise in the house, covering the cage may not work. The Cockatiel can hear its favorite people or TV show, and it continues to call for attention. Turn down some of the noise if you expect the Cockatiel to calm down. If there is more than one Cockatiel in the house, the birds can also be expected to call back and forth to each other just to keep in touch. That's perfectly natural. If you're disturbed by peeping birds, restrict yourself to a single pet Cockatiel.

What if the Cockatiel calls constantly, hour after hour, day after day? It's time to evaluate the amount of time you spend with your pet. Have you gotten distracted with other things? Has play time gradually shrunk to a pitiful 15 or 20 minutes a day? Cockatiels are highly social birds, and they get terribly lonely if they have no one to play with. If you continue to ignore your pet, it could become seriously depressed or lose its tameness.

You can probably fit your Cockatiel back into your schedule without too much trouble. Are you too tired to do anything but watch TV? Turn on the tube, and let the Cockatiel

If you find that you do not have ample time to spend with your Cockatiel, be fair! Get the bird a companion with which it can socialize.

watch with you. All birds enjoy music videos, but Cockatiels seem to have a special fondness for any kind of musical or trendy programming. If you're stretched out flat on the sofa, let the Cockatiel walk over your body. When you eat a nutritious snack or meal, bring the Cockatiel along for a taste. As your energy returns, work on some tricks with the Cockatiel. Swap around the toys in its cage or on the playground.

As you increase the amount of time you spend with your Cockatiel, choose the times when you approach the bird carefully. If it's really screaming, refuse to take the bird out to play until it has calmed down. If you always respond to shrieking by releasing the bird from its cage, it will think that shrieking is the way to get what it wants.

Cockatiels sometimes thrash in their cages in the middle of the night, beating their wings against the bars so loudly that they can wake you up from several rooms away. Once they're thrashing, they may not be able to regain their calm until you turn on the light to show them that everything is OK. For this reason, you should always keep a night light in the room where the Cockatiel sleeps. Some people prefer a slightly brighter light, such as a seven-watt bulb in a small decorator lamp.

You should also try to find out what has frightened the Cockatiel. Some people dismiss the problem as nightmares, but there's often a real intruder in the bird room that's terrifying the Cockatiel. Some possibilities include mice, lizards, spiders, and large cockroaches. Keep the area around the cage scrupulously clean, vacuuming dropped seed every day. Ask a bird specialty store for an insecticide that's safe to use around birds. Eliminate mice with traps, not poison. The lizards are harmless, but you need to remove them if they're scaring the Cockatiel. I simply catch them and drop them outside. Then work on a program of cleaning up the room to eliminate insects, which are probably what attracted the lizard in the first place.

Most Cockatiels don't bite unless they're frightened. If your bird has become a biter, check its wings. Have they grown out, giving the Cockatiel a false sense of power? Trim them back. If the bird continues to bite, evaluate your approach to the bird. Are you moving in soft, gentle motions, approaching from the side so the Cockatiel can see you clearly in one eye, or are you grabbing eagerly like a hungry predator? Are you talking to the bird when you approach, or are you startling it by walking right up without saying a word? Don't feel stupid talking to a bird. The Cockatiel may not understand everything you say, but it will appreciate being treated like a person. When you sneak up on it, you're treating it more like a midnight snack!

To discourage your Cockatiel from biting, tell it, "No!" in a loud, clear voice each time it bites. Don't grab or hit the

Patience and gentle handling are recommended when it comes to discouraging a biting Cockatiel.

bird. The loud "No!" should be enough to startle it into letting go of your flesh. Don't punish the bird. If you're really upset, you can put the bird in its cage for now. However, don't lock the bird up every time it bites. Otherwise, it will think that biting is the way to tell you that it's tired and ready to retire.

The best way to discourage biting is to handle the bird gently and lovingly, so that it learns that it has nothing to fear from you. Scratch its ears, approaching slowly. Offer it a small

There are many opportunities for spending time with your Cockatiel. All efforts will help create and maintain a wonderful relationship that will last for years.

spray of millet from your fingers. Monitor training sessions so that the Cockatiel doesn't get tired or grouchy. You will usually have some warning before a Cockatiel bites. It may hiss, slash the air with its beak, and erect its crest. If it's irritable, let it play alone for awhile. If it's keyed up, distract it with something to chew or a trick that uses its beak. Never, ever tease a Cockatiel. Don't frustrate the bird by eating forbidden treats, such as chocolate or ice cream, when it's around.

As your relationship deepens with your Cockatiel, you will gradually become sensitive to its moods, just as it will become more sensitive to yours. What's more heartwarming than a Cockatiel strutting over to cheer you up, bopping its head against your hand for an ear scratching? As you train your pet, rewarding it with affection and attention for the behaviors you want to reinforce, your Cockatiel will become more loving as it grows more intelligent. You will have trained a pet that the whole family will cherish for many years.

SUGGESTED READING

THE ENCYCLOPEDIA OF COCKATIELS
By George A. Smith
ISBN 0-87666-958-5
TFH PS-743

This excellent book, written on the high school level, is designed to help *all* Cockatiel owners, beginners and experienced aviculturists alike. It covers every important aspect of Cockatiel maintenance, feeding, housing, breeding, and disease control and treatment; in addition, there is a very fine section on Cockatiel genetics and breeder selection.

A STEP-BY-STEP BOOK ABOUT COCKATIELS
By Anmarie Barrie
ISBN 0-86622-453-X
TFH SK-007

This volume, the companion to *A Step-By-Step Book About Training Cockatiels*, touches all the bases of caring for the pet Cockatiel: selection, cages, feeding, diseases, and breeding. The information is presented in simple, easy-to-read English, telling the reader exactly how to enjoy his bird to the fullest while making routine maintenance a pleasure rather than a chore.

PARROTS AND RELATED BIRDS
By Henry J. Bates and Robert L. Busenbark
ISBN 0-87666-967-4
TFH H-912

This is the "bible" for parrot lovers. It has more color photographs and more information than any other single book on the subject. Written primarily for the owner of more than one parrot or parrot-like bird, this is a necessary reference work for serious parrot lovers and keepers. Up-to-date scientific nomenclature and many color photos make this book a treasure to own.

INDEX

Age determination, 15
Aggression, 25
Albino Cockatiel, 9
Attention span, 26, 36
Behavior problems, 46–61
Bird toys, 42, 43
Biting, 27, 29, 30, 57–59
Cage situation, 20
Calling, 52–55
Cinnamon Cockatiel, 9
"Cockatoo" dust (powder), 12, 20
"Come" command, 36, 37
Conditioning, 36
Congenital bald spot, 8, 18
Fright, 57
Handfed Cockatiels, 15–16,, 22
Housebreaking, 39, 40
Keelbone, 17
Ladder game, 29
Life expectancy, 6
Lutino Cockatiel, 8, 18
Millet spray, 24, 36, 59
Mirrors, 43
Nail clipping, 51
Nasal turbinate, 16
Natural environment, 4

Night light, 57
Normal Cockatiel, 6, 7
Nymphicus hollandicus, 4
Objectionable words, 41
Pearly Cockatiel, 9
Pearly Pied Whiteface Cockatiel, 9
Pied (harlequin) Cockatiel, 9
Playpen, 43
Quarantine, 20
Recordings, 37, 38, 44
Selecting, 10–19
Seller's guarantee, 13
Sex differentiation, 6, 14
Sex-linked mutation, 8
Silver Cockatiel, 9
Styptic powder, 46, 51
Talking, 12
Talking, 34–45
Taming, 20–23
Taming area, 23, 24
Training, 34–47
Trick training, 40–46
Vocabulary, 34
Whistling, 44
Whiteface Cockatiel, 9
Wing-clipping, 18, 19, 37, 38, 46–49